DRINKS WITH
THE TOTTERINGS

ANNIE TEMPEST

HE DRINKS WINE · SHE DRINKS WINE...

F

FRANCES LINCOLN LIMITED
PUBLISHERS

Frances Lincoln Limited
4 Torriano Mews
Torriano Avenue
London NW5 2RZ
www.franceslincoln.com

British Library Cataloguing in Publication Data
A catalogue record for this book is available from
the British Library.

ISBN 978-0-7112-3085-9

Printed in China
Bound for North Pimmshire

9 8 7 6 5 4 3

Other Tottering-by-Gently books by Annie Tempest:
Out and About with the Totterings
The Totterings' Desk Diary
The Totterings' Pocket Diary
Available from Frances Lincoln at www.franceslincoln.com

At Home with the Totterings
Tottering-by-Gently Vol III
Available from The Tottering Drawing Room, along with a full range of
Tottering-by-Gently licensed product, at The O'Shea Gallery, No. 4 St James's Street,
London SW1A 1EF (Telephone +44 (0)207 930 5880) or www.tottering.com

Lord Tottering
'Dicky'

Lady Tottering
'Daffy'

Serena

Freddy

Daisy

Gladys Shagpile

Scribble

Slobber

TOTTERING-BY-GENTLY ®
ANNIE TEMPEST

Annie Tempest is one of the top cartoonists working in the UK. This was recognized in 2009 with the Cartoon Art Trust awarding her the Pont Prize for the portrayal of the British Character. Annie's cartoon career began in 1985 with the success of her first book, *How Green Are Your Wellies?* This led to a regular cartoon, 'Westenders' in the *Daily Express*. Soon after, she joined the *Daily Mail* with 'The Yuppies' cartoon strip which ran for more than seven years and for which, in 1989, she was awarded 'Strip Cartoonist of the Year'. Since 1993 Annie Tempest has been charting the life of Daffy and Dicky Tottering in Tottering-by-Gently – the phenomenally successful weekly strip cartoon in *Country Life*.

Daffy Tottering is a woman of a certain age who has been taken into the hearts of people all over the world. She reflects the problems facing women in their everyday life and is completely at one with herself, while reflecting on the intergenerational tensions and the differing perspectives of men and women, as well as dieting, ageing, gardening, fashion, food, field sports, convention and much more.

Daffy and her husband Dicky live in the fading grandeur of Tottering Hall, their stately home in the fictional county of North Pimmshire, with their extended family: daughter Serena, and grandchildren, Freddy and Daisy. The daily, Mrs Shagpile, and love of Dicky's life, Slobber, his black Labrador, and the latest addition to the family, Scribble, Daisy's working Cocker Spaniel, also make regular appearances.

Annie Tempest was born in Zambia in 1959. She has a huge international following and has had eighteen one-woman shows, from Mexico to Mayfair. Her work is now syndicated from New York to Dubai and she has had twelve collections of her cartoons published. *Drinks with the Totterings* is the latest to be published and the first of a new series of collections around a particular theme.

THE O'SHEA GALLERY

Raymond O'Shea of The O'Shea Gallery was originally one of London's leading antiquarian print and map dealers. Historically, antiquarian galleries sponsored and promoted contemporary artists who they felt complemented their recognized areas of specialization. It was in this tradition that O'Shea first contacted *Country Life* magazine to see if Annie Tempest would like to be represented and sponsored by his gallery. In 1995 Raymond was appointed agent for Annie Tempest's originals and publisher of her books. Raymond is responsible for creating an archive of all of Annie's cartoons.

In 2003, the antiquarian side of his business was put on hold and the St. James's Street premises were finally converted to The Tottering Drawing Room at The O'Shea Gallery. It is now the flagship of a worldwide operation that syndicates and licenses illustrated books, prints, stationery, champagne, jigsaws, greetings cards, ties and much more. It has even launched its own fashion range of tweeds and shooting accessories under the label Gently Ltd.

The Tottering Drawing Room at The O'Shea Gallery is a wonderful location which is now available for corporate events of 45–125 people and is regularly used for private dinner parties catering for up to 14 people. Adjacent to St. James's Palace, the gallery lies between two famous 18th century shops: Berry Bros. & Rudd, the wine merchants and Locks, the hatters. Accessed through French doors at the rear of the gallery lies Pickering Place – not only the smallest public square in Great Britain, with original gas lighting, but it was also where the last duel in England was fought. A plaque on the wall, erected by the Anglo-Texan Society, indicates that from 1842–45 a building here was occupied by the Legation from the Republic of Texas to the Court of St. James.

Raymond O'Shea and Annie Tempest are delighted to be able to extend Tottering fans a warm welcome in the heart of historic St. James's where all the original Tottering watercolours can be seen along side a full product and print range.

INTRODUCTION

I am delighted to be writing this introduction to *Drinks with the Totterings* – mainly because my company, Berry Bros & Rudd, can count the Tottering family amongst our most long-standing customers. When the 1st Viscount, Henry 'Parsnip' Tottering, rebuilt Tottering Hall in 1734, the extensive cellars were filled with casks of the finest port, and the quantity of hand blown bottles, complete with the family crest, was such that they gave the name of 'Parsnip Bottles' to the distinctive shape still sought after by collectors today. His grandson was weighed virtually once a month for thirty years on the famous weighing scales in our St James's Street shop. The 4th Viscount was a noted connoisseur, especially of 'Vin de Constance' from South Africa, of which he amassed a famous collection, but it was the 6th Viscount, 'Spotted Dick', who laid down the foundations of the cellar that exists today. Some of the pre-phylloxera claret he bought in the early years of the 20th century still slumbers in quiet corners of the cellars; Imperial Tokay was imported especially for him; he even asked my grandfather, Francis Berry, to create a special liqueur for him to serve as an accompaniment to his heiress wife's famous custard, served hot from flasks on shooting parties at their Scottish estate. With a base of kummel, blue curaçao and crème de menthe, it was greatly enjoyed by the Totterings' guests, but surprisingly never found commercial success when we marketed it as 'Dick's Blister Blaster'.

In recent times the association has continued: the current Lord and Lady Tottering are frequent guests in our dining rooms, and Lady Tottering's nephew, Piers Fitzstonic-Gordons, even enjoyed a brief but eventful period working for us in our Hong Kong shop. Annie Tempest's splendid illustrations seem to me to encapsulate an important truth understood by generations of Totterings: that the finest wines and spirits are far from the scourge of modern society portrayed by our puritan press, but an integral part of a civilized way of life we are in danger of throwing away.

Simon Berry
Chairman, Berry Bros & Rudd, 3 St James's Street, London SW1

Gottcha! That makes it three males and one female..

How on earth can you tell which sex they are?

The first three were after my wine and that one was on the 'phone...

I know what this one is! It's one of those wines
that by-passes your head and goes straight to your legs...

Ah! An aggressive, angular, brawny wine... decadent, volatile... lacking in generosity...

Just one question...

...does it have a criminal record?..

More Pimms, Madam?..

A good reception?...

Yes. Could you send a piano tuner out— I'm afraid a decanter of port got knocked into it...

Dicky! They need some details—age, make and so forth...

It was a 1928 Cockburn that my father put down for me...

THE GUEST FROM HELL GETS A SECOND WIND

THE MALE CHARACTER: Unlike the female, he shows no embarrassment at turning up at a party wearing the same outfit as everyone else...

THE FEMALE CHARACTER: The prudence to reach for a chair and a drink before answering the telephone...

Anybody here own a blue Range Rover?

THE FEMALE CHARACTER
A talent for multitasking, even when at rest...

"We don't eat health foods. At our age we need all the preservatives we can get…"

You must be getting old, Dicky. I saw you look at the wine list before the waitress...

I'm afraid Daffy's bolted straight to the Pimms tent...

Ah ha! The estate agent's philosophy...

...'location is everything'...

1996 © ANNIE TEMPEST.

A woman's life can feel like performing a juggling act whilst riding a unicycle through a ploughed field...

Sometimes we just have to prioritise....

What a perfect day! The sun is out and so are the kids...

We haven't invited our GP to a dinner party for ages. Perhaps we should?

I wouldn't risk it these days...

...He might send some out of hours German locum in his place...

There's something about smart cocktail parties...

I don't know what it is...

but they just make me want to put my gumboots on and eat baked beans..

ANNIE TEMPEST © 1999

"How on earth do people without horse boxes cope with a trip to the bottle bank after a good dinner party?"

"Remind me - was it you or your brother who was killed in the war..?"

What do you make of this cryogenics business, Dicky?

I think being put on ice would be a fate worse than death, old chap...

Imagine being thawed out in 100 years' time to find there was no Cockburn '65 left...

1997 © ANNIE TEMPEST.

"*I wonder if the number of daughters a man's allocated in this life
is in direct proportion to how wicked he was in the previous one...*"

"I believe the red ribbon means she kicks..."

What about this Chardonnay, Mum?

No-too buttery... Aha! This Berry Bros. Sauvignon is light and refreshing - that should fit the bill...

...mmm... the perfect compliment to a box of choccies and a romantic comedy...

Annie Tempest © 2003

"Whoops! I think I'm a little too in touch with my inner Mouton Roths-child..."

GIRLS' NIGHT OUT...

" Emergency services? Two large Bloody Mary's, please..."

It's a naïve domestic Burgundy without any breeding but it's amusingly presumptive..

You are insufferably pretentious, Dicky! Let's see what Mrs. Shagpile makes of it...

Don't tell me – it's definitely over a fiver... it's one of them sophisticated French vino's that don't give you a hangover?..

DOMESTIC GODDESS

Annie Tempest © 2005

"What did you shay went into thish cocktail?.."

"...and this wine is best in volume with a good romantic comedy..."

"Aah, yes - a heady bouquet of dry rot and wet Labrador..."

"Oops! The bubbles have gone up my nose, madam..."

"Frankly, no - I wouldn't like baked bean flavoured crisps with my Petrus '82..."

"Let's have a look - Yup - it's definitely red wine..."

Pour it...

Swig it...

... pour it...

... swig it...

... pour it...

... swig it...

Admire it...

... swirl it about a bit...

... sniff it...

...nod knowingly...

...imbibe it loudly...

... savour the price of it...

YOUNG AT HEART...

...rather more mature in the liver...

YOUNG AT HEART...

... slightly older in other places ...

This wine needs to be given the chance to breathe...

Heavens! Does it?..

Quick – pour me a glass – I'll give it mouth to mouth...

ST. JAMES'S STREET

Boodles and Whites are on the right
As you totter up St. James's
All the rest are on the left
... but I forget their names's ...

A drop more red wine for me but no more for my husband, thankyou - his face is going all blurry...

"Look out! Here comes that chap we used to call the exorcist—
the one who came to dinner and cleared us out of spirits ..."

The 'who's driving tonight' discussion...

I'm pregnant so I'm eating for two...

Lucky you! I'm well past having excuses like that...

...but it's my husband's turn to drive so I'm drinking for two...

Now that you've decided on which wine we're having for dinner, what shall we talk about?

A drop more wine, Daffy?

No thanks, darling – I told you, I'm being good...

...I'm limiting myself to only one glass a night...

"it was *HORRIFYING!*.. There was this dyslexic woman in Whites all in a muddle about which way to pass the port..."

"What's the point of all your hard work in the garden if I'm not allowed to
sit down and enjoy it...."

Searching for the fountain of youth...

The house is tidy. The family's out and I've liberated a good bottle of wine...

The attic's sorted out and I've stuck the last seven years of photos into the album...

Yee-hah!..

My new year's resolution is to finish all the things I've started and never finished...

Now. Where did I put that box of photographs I'd started sorting into years...

Ooh! Look! Half a bottle of Baileys... I'd better start by finishing this...

"Are we running late or have we forgotten we were due for dinner at 8 with the Eameaux-Chavs?.."

Do you like my arrangement, Martin?

It's magnificent, Daffy — but you can't see your husband...

No. And he can't see how much of his best wine I'm drinking...

" My quack tells me there's nothing he can give me to stop me having any more grandchildren..."

Imagine if children were like vintage wines, James...

You could store them away in the cellar for twenty years...

...and they'd reach maturity all on their own...

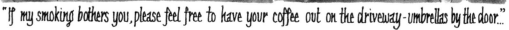

"If my smoking bothers you, please feel free to have your coffee out on the driveway - umbrellas by the door..."

"Apparently this IS the smoking area…"

"Burgundy makes you think silly things... Bordeaux makes you talk about them... ...and Champagne makes you do them..."

"I love all things 'Retro' – that's why I still smoke and drink"

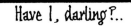

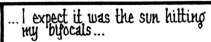

Dicky Tottering was quite put out in White's last week...

an old chum went up to him after dinner and said...

"I say, old chap - aren't we both dead?..."

Ah! Morning, Mrs Shagpile – scrubbing the floors in my wine cellars, are you!

Yes – I'm well into my spring cleaning, Lord T...

...and I've had every one of these dusty old bottles out and given them a good soap down in my bucket...

Nothing nicer after a good party than kicking off your shoes...

having a quiet night cap...

...and letting your stomach muscles out...

THE FEMALE CHARACTER: A *deep sense of gratitude for the institution of the Gentleman's Club...*

Mine's a Grant and Lang...   Mine's a Holland and Holland...   Mine's a Gin and Tonic...

THE SHOOT DINNER

PULL!

A Good Nose...

A Good Nose...

" I take it you had a good evening at your club, dear..."

You go ahead - I'm waiting for Trenchfoot - we're lunching together...

Ah! Tottering! Decided not to wait for Willie, eh!

Just remembered I went to his memorial two weeks ago...

"...The future's not what it used to be, Dicky..."

Nonsense, Daffy - Dicky's an excellent cook - I remember he once made us all a wonderful dinner...

Oh, yes! I remember - it didn't appear until ten to midnight...

so do I - and we'd all had so many champagne cocktails that our taste buds had passed out...

"I think it's time we went to the bottle bank, darling..."

"3rd Tuesday of the 5th month - is that this pink bin with purple spots for Champagne corks and take away curry containers only?."

"To hell with convention! I'm staying and you can pass the port cross-country, Dicky!..."

Some red wines are best enjoyed with beef or lamb...

...and others are perfect with chocolates, magazines and a sloppy Labrador...

CORK OVER !...

DANGEROUS	SAFER	SAFEST
Should you be eating that?	There are some carrots in the fridge...	Here. Have a nice glass of wine...
What have you been doing all day?	I hope you didn't over-do it today...	Here. Have a nice glass of wine...
Are you wearing that?	Wow! You look good in grey...	Here. Have a nice glass of wine...

Visit THE TOTTERING DRAWING ROOM
at No. 4 St. James's Street
LONDON SWIA IEF

TOTTERING BRAND

Cartoonist **Annie Tempest's** famous world of **Tottering-by-Gently**, which appears weekly in *Country Life* magazine, has spawned a wonderful range of original and stylish gifts. Her main characters, Daffy and Dicky and their extended family living at the crumbling stately pile, Tottering Hall, provide the vehicle for her wickedly observant humour covering all aspects of the human condition.

The Tottering range of gifts is suitable for everyone with a sense of fun.
Gifts include:
a large range of Signed Numbered Edition Prints, as well as Digital Prints on Demand (any Annie Tempest image produced as a digital print), books, diaries, greeting cards, postcards, tablemats, coasters, trays, noteblocks, wooden jigsaws, playing cards, mugs, paper bins, silk ties and braces, weekly planners and much more – we even have our own brand of Tottering-by-Gently Champagne . . .

You can telephone us on 01732 866041 for a catalogue, order from our secure website at www.tottering.com or when you are next in London, pop into The Tottering Drawing Room at The O'Shea Gallery, at No.4, St. James's Street, SW1A 1EF, where all the products are available.

www.tottering.com

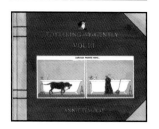

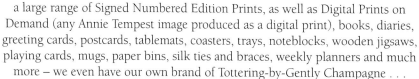

How on earth do people without horse boxes cope with trips to the bottle bank?..

Slobber! Scribble! Stop that!

Oh! Leave them alone, Dicky!..

That's my pre-wash cycle...

THE FEMALE CHARACTER: The prudence to reach for a chair and a drink before answering the telephone...

"...The future's not what it used to be, Dicky..."

Appreciating a fine Claret...

Enjoying an ordinary Claret...

Some red wines are best enjoyed with beef or lamb...

...and others are perfect with chocolates, magazines and a sloppy labrador...

GALLERY OF TOTTERING DESIGNS – Selected product images

"Are we running late or have we forgotten we were due for dinner at 8 with the Exmeaux-Chavs?.."

Is it that time already?

I've had every one of those dusty old bottles of yours out and given them a good soak down in my bucket...

"If my smoking bothers you, please feel free to have your coffee out on the driveway - umbrellas by the door."

HE DRINKS WINE · SHE DRINKS WINE...

A drop more red wine for me but no more for my husband, thankyou - his face is going all blurry...

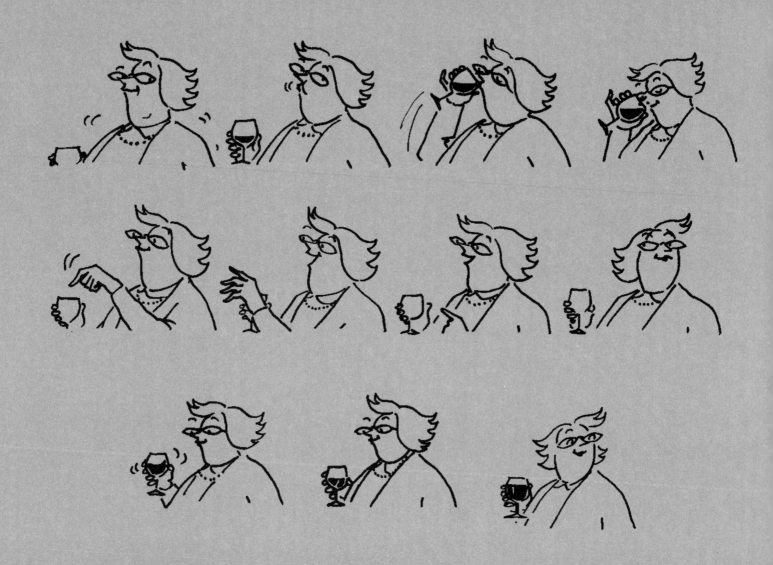